The Airing Cupboard

Ruth Carr

SUMMER PALACE PRESS

First published in 2008 by

Summer Palace Press
Cladnageeragh, Kilbeg, Kilcar, County Donegal, Ireland

arts council
of Northern Ireland

© Ruth Carr, 2008

Printed by Nicholson & Bass Ltd.

A catalogue record for this book is available
from the British Library

ISBN 978-0-9552122-7-7

This book is printed on elemental chlorine-free paper

for Pete and Vivien Patea

Acknowledgments

Some of the poems in this book have previously appeared in: *Fortnight; HU; The SHOp* and in the anthologies *The Backyards of Heaven* (Poetry from Newfoundland and Ireland, 2003); *Out to Lunch* (Poets from Dublin's lunchtime reading series, 2002); *A Trail of Silver Papers* (Shalom House Poets, 2007) and *My Mother Wore a Yellow Dress* (Carrickfergus Council Louis MacNeice Centenary, 2008). One poem has been recorded on CD, *Write to Be Heard* (Poetry in Motion, New Belfast Community Arts Initiative, 2008).

I wish to acknowledge with gratitude the writers Louis Muinzer, Mary Twomey, Elizabeth Kemp and Alastair Browne, who are no longer with us.

The sequence 'Calling the Register' was written with the help of an Arts Council of Northern Ireland Support for the Individual Artist Bursary.

Biographical Note

Ruth Carr was born in Belfast in 1953. Among other jobs, she has worked as an education welfare officer, library assistant and associate lecturer for the Belfast Institute of Further and Higher Education. She produced *The Female Line*, an anthology of poetry, fiction and drama, for the N.I. Women's Rights Movement (1985); compiled the contemporary women's fiction section of *The Field Day Anthology of Irish Writing (IV/V)* and co-edited *HU* poetry magazine for a number of years until its final issue in 2003. She is a member of the Word of Mouth poetry collective. Her first collection, *There is a House*, was published in 1999.

CONTENTS

slow turning	11
When she told me	12
Broken Record	13
ἐκ τούτου / From this	14
Calling the Register	
First Job	15
Education Welfare	16
Failure	17
Careless talk	18
Tedium	20
Victor	21
Growing up	22
Black taxi	23
One was like her, the other one loved her	24
Crumb	26
Intermediate Treatment	27
Your own good	28
Mrs Chillingworth	30
Breaking the rules	31
Extra-curricular at the Ormeau Baths	32
Some places you just don't feel safe in	33
John Ramprakash	34
He saw her in the Molesworth Gallery	36
The Blessing	38
Helping ourselves	39

Auxiliary	40
Resistance	42
Ley lines	43
The year before he learns to drive	44
Going into the millennium with my dad	46
Insurmountable	47
Perspective	48
Burning Sage	49
Warsaw Journey	50
In this poem	52
Catching	54
Finding Mendel's garden	55
Woman jumps from high-rise	56
Glasnost	57
Flowers for Ruth	58
Diogenes in Wolseley Street	59
Her parting shot	60
Sacred household	62
Grace	63
The Airing Cupboard	64

slow turning

knock the door
no answer

no brush of a hand on a curtain
no mist on the pane

the key fits but the lock is stiff
slow turning between thumb and finger

the mainspring gives
unpractised hinges sing

light floods the narrow floor
hover there a moment on the threshold

a footfall on the stair or from next door
it concertinas time

and you are small again
climbing the steep steps left foot first

to find her, patient on the bed
waiting   between worlds

if you could write it now
you'd let her go from there

When she told me

When she told me
not to go so ram-stam
it was all in my own hands the way the seam would grow –

When she told me
to swing from the door-frame
that scrubbing the floor on my hands and knees would bring it on –

When she told me
in letters from home
my name could no longer be spoken under their roof –

When she told me
promptly, no!
I could not come back home –

When she told me
with mild surprise
peering into cupboards, I was really quite tidy –

When she told me
the happiest bit
was when she knew we were both at school –

When she told me in a whisper
to be sure
to throw out the dirt-trap of a mat at their front door –

She was telling me things
I took in like washing off the line
folded and stacked in a basket

waiting to be smoothed out
in her absence
with the gradual airing of time.

Broken Record

The needle's darting pain
as it skids across the vinyl like a drunk on ice
is something like the stab we made at marriage.

The groove you wallowed in was also mine.
My needling voice the backing to your
slow repeating vocal, over and over.

There comes a time you realise
the needle doesn't have to keep on sticking,
that you don't have to listen out of habit.

But first you have to hear the breaking point,
blunt against the bone inside your ear – it screams
at you to raise the needle's arm and not your own.

Eight long playing years.
A compilation album of our hits and misses,
the closing song your favourite from the big O –

It's Over

ἐκ τούτου / From this
for Mr Young

But for you, fresh from college,
augmenting the classics team;
but for the school allowing a class of one
– how could they sanction it now?
But for the head down, shoulder by shoulder desks,
the craft we settled in, to labour with Heracles,
you steering a course line by line,
setting sail with Homer.

Without your gift for navigation
leading me into the waters of translation
to find my own depth in the Aegean.
Without your concern that we try,
at least try, to think inside the language,
the light spilling through the sash window
gracing the open page. Without this beginning
with you and the wing-footed Hermes

my path would have been the more travelled one,
might never have found my own tongue.

Calling the Register

don't swallow your own lies,
    'The sick primer', Miroslav Holub

First job

Straight from Uni, rose-tinted as they come,
not a decent outfit to my name –
which happened to be Hooley, none too popular

up the top of the Shankill and beyond
where I hoofed it round Highfield, a pack
of hungry dogs in tow, wove through

Blackmountain's bricked-up sixties high-rise
and legged it down Springfield, oblivious of harm.
The sheer naivety of it.

Black-taxied it back to town
to tick absent boxes, despatch officious letters,
softened top and bottom with my scrawl.

The sheer futility of it.
Saved from all harm, from all threats
by sheer ignorance.

The sheer arrogance of it. To think
I could make a difference to lives
so inextricably knotted.

I didn't know how to do this job.
I didn't know how to catch kids.
I only knew that I

had somewhere else to go and they did not.

Education Welfare

Looking back, she must have been the age
that I am now. In framed unblinking eyes
I glimpse the girl she saw in me –

long-haired, street-ignorant and lost.
Which may have prompted her
to corner me inside the stationery cupboard,

and opening her tightly lidded heart
along with her bag,
divulge this tip:

*I find it best
when calling at clients' doors
never to cross the threshold.*

She smiled conspiratorially.
I remember, I smiled too,
not seeing what would come.

*A dab of scent just there beneath your nose
will do the trick … the state some people live in.
Here, take this,*

pressing a perfume sample into my palm
she lifted a wad of forms and left me pondering
if this particular fragrance wafted a subtle subtext,

Je Reviens

Failure

I knew in my bones if I'd been the one
appointed to sit where Mr Jackson sat
behind his desk, I'd be exactly like him:
unable to keep control or entertain or switch to
Mr Hyde; laughed at for expecting them to care.
Because he never raised his hand, refused
to put them down, they had no time for him;
did what they liked in his class and he just
kept his head down. They had won.
Or was it the system defeated them both?

Careless talk

the catchphrase of that time,
rang true the day
I knocked on Sammy's door.

His dad opened it wide,
invited me in for a drink
which I declined

telling him his son was at risk,
mixing with big boys
in derelict flats

stealing lead pipes
and selling them,
beaking off school.

He slammed the door
and through the wood
reverberated

each blow
the force of his hand
the screams of his son.

Sammy returned to school
a few days later.
Then slipped back

to business.
Nobody noticed.
One less trouble-maker.

I talked to him once
up in the flats in Blackmountain.
He simply shrugged

his slender shoulders
and blinked his eyes;
twinkly, watchful eyes.

I never went back to his door.

Tedium

Some of them used to wait in the derelict flats.
Out of boredom
made gable ends their blackboard,
left me messages:

We R (•)(•) U

Texting before its time, really.
Like hide and seek
half wanting to be caught,
half wanting to be noticed
for their absence,
for their ingenuity.

Victor

I pick you for not standing out,
the boy in the background
vanishing before the school gates,
evaporating into chill air,
the mist on Blackmountain.

Victor, unimpressed by school,
too many hoops of rules.
School unimpressed by you,
took you for a fool, didn't see
how you ran rings round

everyone, survived the dark days
juggling truth with fiction,
out-manoeuvred meanness,
side-stepped harm.
Victor, in more than name.

Growing up

It comes as a shock but no surprise
when you flaunt a ruby in my face
the week you officially leave
(although you were never there).

We are equals, your look says,
your ring as good as mine
(in some ways Woolworths better).

In years to come I'll take mine off,
call myself a fool and think of you,
Laura, making it up as you go.

Black taxi

The clemency of rain that morning,
gradually seeping through.
When I opened the door

warmth rising off worn leather,
misting my glasses, the press
of squeezing in, thigh to thigh,

water dripped down my neck
as I turned to take in mother and daughter,
half smiling uncomfortably.

And I smiled too, doubts like the drips
blurring our hampered views – me with my boxes to tick,
you on your weekly visit out to the Maze.

One was like her, the other one loved her

Answering the door in his Y-fronts
he more than smiled, he
smirked at me.

The blue-eyed boy, eighteen,
who'd done his stint in Borstal,
learnt the lot.

She worried about the gun they'd given him
to mind a prisoner's wife. Worried more
about the young wife and her son.

She had good reason.
He soon met harder men than he could ever be,
had to run for his life.

The younger one was different.
His dad watched from a distance,
worried he'd beak too.

She couldn't see the point of books,
all those lines that let you down
and showed you up.

The numbers on her bin were upside down,
her life was inside out
and talked about.

She couldn't see the mountain out her window
anymore, couldn't feel it
lifting like an alp.

The younger son was different,
kept his head down like his dad.
Let on he didn't notice anything,

stayed there like the mountain
when she took to drink. Added up the bills
and tipped her vodka down the sink.

Crumb

Leaving the flats
a window above unlatches
and down flops my hat,
the one my mother had crocheted
like a moss-covered teacosy.

I took it for a good sign
that she bothered at all,
that she called out to me
Miss, you might be needing this,
before she let it fall
from finger and thumb.

Intermediate Treatment

Every boy referred there got on well.
Loved being on first name terms with the staff,
loved the smoke breaks,
loved making things that worked,
loved being able to talk about their lives for real.

The problems re-emerged when they returned.
School was just the same. They didn't fit.
Rejects expected to mark time for their absences
in no-hope, non-exam seats at the back
Just keep the volume down or you'll get this!

Was it preparation for the times – a state
of containment? The streets won every day.
More dangerous, more inviting. More potential
for success at being a hard man,
for human failure.

Your own good

You watch,
wary as the fledgling in the hawthorn at the gate
as the door swings shut behind me.

And with each step I think of your step
desperate, deliberate
your delicate bones, my own unbroken body.

I think of your child-soft head as we peg
your life out between us,
your unheld, half-grown hand

taking the medication
measured out
from the metal tray.

And with each breath I take it in – you wanting
to down the moon in one whole go
wanting to pick the stars

from the black cloth of night
and wrap yourself in it
for good.

My hand on the gate
I turn and wave. The bird
stops trying its handful of notes

and I, who never do, pray it isn't an omen,
pray that you are grounded somewhere
safe enough to shelter, safe enough to breathe.

You don't wave back, why would you?
Another person leaving, nothing new,
nothing good.

Mrs Chillingworth

We never met.
Whenever we spoke on the phone
I pictured you holding my latest referral, pen
in hand, half smiling. Could hear it in your voice,
the gentle humour masking exasperation.

You were the end of the line
and I imagined you still
as a boulder in a bay of little fish,
some of them turned belly-up,
some sheltering in your shadow.

You were the end of the line
and I expected miracles from your hands.
You were the fisher of boys and girls,
you could cast your spell and draw them in.
This was the catch that mattered.

But there you were at the end of the line
each time, telling me yes, you already knew;
that this was the tip above water;
that there was a history to delve into;
that they were much further out and no lifeboats.

You were the voice at the end of the line
sounding the depths of this shallow job,
the short leash of its anchor.
Your tone neither bitter nor despairing,
simply, calmly aware.

Breaking the rules

One night I go up late
to call on someone's father after work.
The place is charged with life,
kids flitting about under cover of dark
between a car in flames and a skip burning.
Shouts, things breaking and a flash of concern
when they see me there where I shouldn't be.
And then alarm in a mother's eyes
when she opens the door.
Fear that I might break the rule of silence
she's maintained around her husband's heart –
he'd take another attack if he found out.

She promises that Malcolm will go back,
swears it on her life.
And he does.
I watch for him next morning on the steps.
He ambles down and in we go –
the first time he's set foot in school all year.
It doesn't last.
The V.P. takes exception to his jacket – it is leather.
Don't come back to school without full uniform!
It works a treat for both the school and boy.

So I stand at the terminus and reflect.
They'll never buy a blazer, not for three months.
No point in bothering with court.
No point in disturbing the peace of his father's heart.

Extra-curricular at the Ormeau Baths

If I had known the Baths were destined for a change of use,
to house a never-ending string of art, a gallery;

that there would come a time when only the walls stayed standing,
no longer washed by the water that washed us clean;

I would have paid more attention to detail, to the particular
steamy whiff of the limey chlorine, the slant of doors,

to the cubicles down each side, the well-worn tiles. But
all I remember now is you pouring bile in my ear

while I waved to your son and daughter, lithe as eels
(that was part of your problem, their limitless grace)

as they slipped through their bodies, dived through space
into a buoyancy, a resilience, their faces at last beaming:

supported briefly in this house of baths, this gallery,
the weight of your resentment suspended, for one afternoon at least.

It all came back full circle
at the press photographers' exhibition, pictures of the past.

Queues to get in – almost like somewhere foreign
or queuing in the old days for a bath.

I entered the water of memory, soon out of my depth
drifting from one searing photograph to the next.

Remembered your desperation, how it was back then,
unable to lead your children out of the dark.

Some places you just don't feel safe in

As far as I know, nothing worse happened there
than anywhere else.

A mix of maisonettes, flats and semis,
some of them burnt and bricked-up,
most of them lived in quietly, not much work.

Round the back, between them and the hill,
a deep green gash of a drop.

Imagined the ground giving way entirely,
a bottomless pit of god-knows-what
under bracken, flag iris and bog.

Couldn't help hearing the faint whingeing
of a dog without its master.
Like wearing heels you can't run in, like
entering a trap. Only the one way in there,
and on foot, a long way back.

John Ramprakash

i

From the lash of your mother's tongue
for being your father's son
you ran
hid in bunkers, burnt-out houses, down entries

and one time up in the roofspace until she cornered you.
Off school for once for a reason –
you couldn't run.
She took his absence out on you.

And you withdrew,
watched the world with unrevealing eyes,
didn't speak, didn't exactly lie.
I saw you smile sometimes with Victor, your beaking pal.

That night: two thirteen-year-olds
crossing late seventies Belfast after dark,
asking for me by name around the Holy Land –
living proof of something good that you found my door.

I took you in, praised your crazy enterprise.
Later, after tea and toast and grave doubts
about my taste in music that made you wonder why
exactly you had come,

I walked you back to the City Hall,
put you both on the last bus
half hoping, half pretending
I'd see you back in school.

I sent you home.

ii
John Ramprakash of the sad, sad eyes
Tell me this and tell me no lies
Did you do it, then? Did you make it through your teens?
Did you join the British Army, did you realise your dreams?

Did they make you mean and tough? Did they send you to the Gulf?
Did you run when it got rough? Did you feel you'd had enough?
Did you finally get your license? Did you get your HGV?
Did you get to be a Yorkie like the advert on TV?

Tell me, John, did you make it through those years?
Through the peaceless eighties, the hurting and the fear?
What about your sister? What about your mum?
And what about Victor? Are you still on the run?

John Ramprakash of the enigmatic smile
Are your hands on the wheel? Are you eating up the miles?
Do you see in the mirror your own long-distance self?

Are you on the road right now to somewhere else?

He saw her in the Molesworth Gallery

in another room,
not the exhibition he had come to view.
Rib-deep in water, only a necklace –
the red coral he'd carried back from Corsica
when they were unknown quantities to each other,
could hardly bear to part.

It was her all right.
Hair straying from its clasp,
head tilted, resting against one hand,
the way she'd look elsewhere,
one elbow anchored to the side,
fingers trailing in the rise and fall.

For one unhemmed-in moment
he imagined her a double life,
saw her briefly through the artist's eyes,
believed it possible.
What did he feel? Not jealousy, not doubt,
a kind of awe, a kind of incredulity.

And when he showed her a printout
she too was mystified, accused him
of playing a trick. Bemused
to think that she had somewhere such a twin,
or perhaps there lived her likeness
in someone else's head.

There she was laid bare,
the boney cave between her breasts,
the cantabile curve of her body.
Entirely herself, an unknown quantity again,
as his foot strayed over the threshold
into another room, another frame.

The Blessing
for Pat and Amy

If I could cut the pattern on the bias
of the cloth, run a steady seam and turn
the hem by hand so no stitch shows;

if I could fit the garment to become
the one it dressed, a blessed second skin,
its wearing easy;

I'd make for you the coat she made for me
when years ago I stood and watched the rails tremble,
walked the threadbare lanes in a low mist.

I recognise it now, her maker's skill:
choosing a Donegal tweed with a haze
of lavender, a touch of sage in the weave,

tucking into the seam a secret pocket
and stowing there against my bony breast
a space for love to bloom.

If I could make you this, I'd twist the thread
with wax to make it last, to make each button hold
and hug you fast whatever road you go.

Helping ourselves

The unfed child in her shoots out a hand
to claim the only morsel on the plate.
I know because it sometimes lurches forward
in me too – a blurting out of want dismissed
as greed, that simply needs the emptiness to go.

I fill the plate and we eat our way from one
side to the other, talk with our mouths full,
drop niceties with crumbs onto the carpet.
Even leave some over for the rest. Full enough
by now to sense there's plenty more to come.

Auxiliary

Our paths crossed just the once.
The Jubilee Ward of the City in '79,
labouring to function under renovation.

All us women giving birth in curtained cubicles
behind plastic-sheeted doors in the one,
hermetically sealed, delivery room.

Staff under duress. The week before, a woman
had let her newborn slip – so no more presenting the baby
on mother's breast, no more guests.

Unaccompanied, each in our own rhythm, we moaned or bit
our tongues in gingham isolation as footsteps, cling-wrapped
in what looked like shower caps, shuffled past

never stopping except to ask *how frequent now, pet?*
Pointless to hope for a birthing pool, to apply my vague
grasp of breathing techniques, or try and ease

the Asian woman's cries with water music.
More like the Ride of the Valkyries, hellbent, spinning out of
control in a downward spiral, this was the stuff of the void.

And yet, in spite of everything misread; being put
to bed for the night, given tablets just as the waters broke;
in spite of doubts and drips and the drug-filled needle;

in spite of the birth plan screwed up tight in my fist;
in spite, most of all, of my shock, my primal fear,
the baby was on course, unmarred.

That was when I reached for something human,
something to grab on to in such undertow, and you
caught hold of my hand and held it firm. Even though

they wanted you to get on with your job of clearing up
behind them, you stayed by, you didn't let me go.
And that was all it took to keep afloat, your steady hand.

May I cross someone's path as you did mine.

Resistance

All the sweet-lined promises from here
to the dark wood door can make no difference.
His face is set to shatter, not wash clear
in scalding tears. His body hunched like a cat's,
weighted against all odds: teachers; parents;
rules, all pointing one-way-only down this path
he will not go.

                His nine years' hard-line stare
takes me back to Mr Thompson's desk. Wedged
between its leg and the edge of his chair
I stared him in the eye until the dredged
forget-me-not blue was all I could see.
Not drowning but staring him through,
I surfaced there, and in that instance I knew
I would not go over his waiting knee.

Ley lines

Let us not burden children with too much learning.
Enough that they know the world is round,
that every line meets itself eventually.

That going far enough north becomes south,
far enough east becomes west
and that people are good in part, the world over.

That what you give out comes back to you.
Enough that they know every unknown road
will have its learning curve.

That the ground under foot
like the stars overhead
will finally bring you home.

The year before he learns to drive

When the primitive speakers rattle like plates
as the bass floods through,
filling the car with a river so strong
I'm glad I've the wheel to hold on to,

my son simply smiles and taps my arm to note
some class guitar riff, some sweet solo.

From Iron Maiden to Arctic Monkeys to the Foals,
from being about my height to way taller
and still rising, all in a couple of years,
his blitzkrieg of a journey.

We turn at the end of our road, past a fence
with flowers rotting. Three boys his age
drove their ride-for-the-night right into it,
without turning,
straight from the garage they'd robbed,
without stopping.

Without believing they could, one of them died.

He is not at sea like me with this flood.
It's part of the way things keep changing,
keep claiming his heart, keep pushing
a new slant with every turn in the road.

I brake at the lights and catch him
singing along with Snow Patrol:

You'll not be around forever, girl...

On our left the paving stones
that pillowed another young man's head last night
as he gulped his final breath.

…You gotta grab life with both hands.

Suddenly conscious that he is the music
filling the space in this car, flooding it
with energy. That crammed into this
moment between lights, between the heavy bass
and his superlatives for the Ulster Hall
as the best concert hall in the universe,

between red and green,
before whatever's next, is this
indelible pressing of who he is to me,
who he will always be.

Going into the millennium with my dad

Today he says
in a voice bereft of feeling,
I wish the war would end.

Sometimes he brings me there,
down, down, where I become as doubtful
as himself about our kind.

Today he's as far away as he was then,
eighteen or eighty, North Africa or Nursing Home –
little difference in the end.

Today he stares right through me
waiting for the All Clear
as I wait with him, to let in the New Year.

Insurmountable

Minnie makes it round the block in eighty seconds flat.
I count each time she passes where we sit,
father and daughter, pondering insurmountables:

>   where my mother has gone,
>   how you will break out of here.

Minnie moves as smoothly as a tight-rope walker,
balancing a book inside her head, one I've never read,
nor ever will. When it comes my time I'll shamble.

Months later, still her feet keep stepping to their call
even though her body's leather-strapped against her will,
to save her face from a battering.

She's started falling for the walls, falling
without hesitation at last,
for the opening arms of her lover.

Like Dorothy of the songbird voice
crooning softly from the cage of her chair;
like my father, dreaming of pissing outside

on the lawn where it says Keep Off;
she wants to walk again,
she wants to waltz.

Perspective
Tom Dowdie 1919-2001

The further down the years you went
the more you stumbled back:

desert rats in rat holes,
minefields, missing limbs;

and further back
the bridge, drum-black with boots;

the night with shots,
lifted from your cot in search of arms.

The one true note you held
papery thin, wedged between the field

of human conflict and your heart,
familiar hand and voice

your little sister's letter
sent from home.

You carried it through everything.
Ordinary words that tell me now

what matters,
what remains.

Burning Sage

He turns into a little snowman and refuses to melt
                    'Ghetto', Michael Longley

The Cherokees believed that every plant
contained a cure. The wild blue iris
mixed with beeswax for abrasions.
Willow bark or lady's slipper root for pain.
They still burn sage to clear the air of evil.
Smudging, it's called, with a bundle
of sagebrush tied up like a wand.
But some can burn the sage without a flame.
Words on the page like buffalo honouring
the plain with their skin, their meat, their bone.
The print of their ghost hooves as clear
as the snow on a small boy's hair,
still standing there, refusing to disappear.

Warsaw Journey
for Maura

It was probably a sign –
the bus to Dublin taking a detour inland to beat
the tailback, scraping down leafy lanes
at a wild rate of knots.

It was probably a sign –
finger too swollen to wear what your heart
carries still, the ring you lost
between taxi and plane.

It was probably a sign –
hauling our bags up four floors
to open a deep-set pane
onto trees and a fountain.

It was probably a sign –
that even with Misia as guide, it was hard to find,
that cavernous fort, dark and damp
where treasures were being unpacked, precariously
hung for the exhibition.

It was probably a sign –
that the Irish and German guests
were asked to come late to the launch,
returning to find it transformed,
row upon row of soft faces lit up and listening.

It was probably a sign –
the next day, leaving our shoes at the door,
our feet felt at home as we knelt to picture our way
in the house of Dakini,
where we opened our mouths and sang.

It was probably a sign –
our journeys finding their endpoint at a mass grave;
side by side, Irish and German, we all tried
to absorb it – uncountable number,
not one of them full grown.

It was probably a sign –
how easily we crossed the language barrier
how easily we read each other's hands, how
easily we waltzed in the hostel bar to youthful stares.

It was probably a sign –
their parting gift to draw the tables close,
dress them with flowers and make
a feast of breaking bread with you and me.

It was probably a sign –
that you brought home a handful of angels,
a horde of images; that I brought home
a fish blue-glazed in a handmade dish.

They were probably all signs
that both of us were ripe for our own journeys.
You, to scale high walls and unearth skills
stored deep, to fly in the face of four corners.
Me to tend the tethered horse left wintering too long.

In this poem

You are turned towards me, naked, sleeping.
I am watching, wanting to be the sheet,
the air around you, the first rays of light
to find you, wanting to fill your eyes
when you wake. I am learning you by osmosis.
I breathe you in, the heat of your skin
as we lie on the white bed in the square room,
its lazy eye over Besançon.

And now I want to ask you, is this how
you remember it? I don't want to know
that it is ordinary, that you can't
recall the way my hair grew daily more
dishevelled because you asked me not to
unplait its weave of confetti and petals.

I want you to say yes, even if you don't
remember the warning shriek
of peacocks, war-weary on the battlements.
Say you can smell the red earth rising
into the rain, the tower we sheltered in
– its slits on the world embroidered with weeds –
seeing unseen from our eyrie.

I want us to sit again in the train
taking us higher into the hills;
breakfast on yoghurt and cereal straight
from the box as woods chug by. To step off
anywhere, take a room in a hamlet
where no one speaks English. Where you can lean
out the window and bite off the roof tiles
like gingerbread, or count the rats in their dozens
under the bridge. Where we can fall
again on a broken-backed bed and not care
about anything more than being here
in this, our field of gold, our sunlit garden.

Catching
April 2001

In this recurring dream
doors are rattling
a culled seal is bleeding a poem
wordlessly into the ice
a child is running upstairs nursing
an armful of snow to save from the thaw

and I am reciting names like a string of pearls
feeling the pull of the thread through every element
how smoke from burning flesh
carries on the wind
our own contaminated words
catching like sheep's wool on barbed wire.

Finding Mendel's garden

He would have gone on failing quietly,
brilliant though he was, first
as a priest, then teacher, scientist, even as a monk.
The kind of man who clammed up on paper
giving too-awkward answers
righter than the ones the cloth required,
writing him off as poor,
but not completely.

He would have gone on failing
but for the shape of a leaf
returning him to his nature
like walking out of shadow into light.

For years we have wondered how his pea plants grew
in the narrow plot ordained within the walls
that gave back darkness –
not knowing his natural choice was to plant
his heart in a south-facing bed
below the study window, the monks waving to him,
wishing the words would flower before their eyes
like Mendel's garden.

Woman jumps from high-rise

More often than not
the lift was out of order
so they climbed in step
one handle of the shopper each
floor after floor
as natural as one breath
after the other.

It knocked the breath
clean out of her
when he went –
no foot to fall in line with
no hand to partner hers
and though the bag weighed less
it felt like more
climbing to the door that
she could beat and beat against
and know there'd be no answer.

Only one.
To pull the worn, serge trousers
over her skirt
not just for modesty,
something of him to hold on to
as she jumped.

Glasnost
Moscow, November 1986

On the steps of one of Stalin's monstrous skyscrapers
two women in ill-fitting overcoats
stoop to shovel the frozen snow
for better-heeled feet on pilgrimage from the West.
Packed between fabric and bone, fistfuls of old
propaganda to fend off their country's cold shoulder.

From the warmth of the coach I cannot tell
how numb their rag-bandaged fingers must be,
heads, hands, backs bent to their task.
The snow begins again and long grey strands
work free from one woman's headscarf.
How swiftly they freeze with her breath.

In perfectly accented English, the guide
for our group explains, sighing dramatically:
It's too sad, old women like these,
they still think their country needs them to be like men.

Mothers of Russia, who swung hammers,
drove tractors, raised beams and dug graves,
you cannot read the fine print against your hearts.
Perestroika has cleared the Cold War path, is
clearing a path for your daughters back to the sink,
back to the vacant gaze of the cattle ring.

Our guide from the Party regrets, as she
repaints her lips: *They just won't re-educate.*

Already they are forgetting your beautiful strength,
already you have become an embarrassment.
Go home, old women.
You who do not know how not to toil,
go home and freeze behind doors,
not here, not out in the open.

Flowers for Ruth
in memory of Ruth Priestley, August 2004

Letting out the dog before the house wakes up,
I stand and listen in the thinning dark.
The plants are listening too, but all I hear
is the dog, her wet nose at my hand,
all I fasten on are flowers among the weeds.
Your kind of flowers that blossom anywhere,
the ones I picked that day to lay alongside
countless armfuls of love and grief for you.

And now, as first light fingers the burnt orange lace
of Donegal monbretia, heartening hard berries
of St John's wort, I press the scent from lavender
and watch rays warm the daisies opening in response:
bright as their namesake, your daughter,
bright as her mother's brimming light.

Diogenes in Wolseley Street
for Jan

Not much bigger than a tub, the boxroom where he squatted,
the spit of Miss Watson, my first and final ballet teacher, reminding me
of the way they were both simultaneously sinuous and substantial.

Leaning long and doggedly against the straight-backed chair
beneath the skylight, waiting for a rest between your medical texts,
he marked time for your bow.

We occupied the attic next to him. Your bed in the high corner,
my mattress on the floor attempting la vie bohémienne,
achieving only a chill from the gale blowing under the door.

With a regularity which gradually came unstrung,
you joined Diogenes in his room and made him sing,
like Moses striking water from a rock.

You brought me in there once.
I watched you lay the bow across his strings, extract a music
deeper than the bold Socratic chat you named him for.

The calmest concentration on your brow
drew up from the cage of his ribs, his cavernous belly,
a slip of a girl,

an Iphigenia pining for her home, her sister,
mother, brother, even the father who traded her life
for a wind to blow him to war.

Out from the wood between your knees and fingertips
her voice uncoiled its grief in tune with yours,
travelled down the stairwell like a mist and settled there –

a smokescreen
between the girl that Diogenes knew
and the rest of the world.

Her parting shot

He doesn't speak to us.
Years now since our plans to raise the roof
which he opposed –
later went and raised his own roof higher.

So when I found what seemed
to be his cat on our side of the hedge,
splayed out, not moving
and our cat sitting satisfied,

it didn't look too good
and I was tempted to leave her by the road.
But when I lifted her
stiff and still-warm body, I found

my feet were walking her to her door,
which meant putting her down
on the pavement while I fiddled
with the bolts to open his gate.

I delivered her wrapped in plastic
into his arms. And all he said was
he'd been expecting it,
her age, her deafness, nearly blind.

She was a cat who liked to travel by night
wherever pleased her,
would not be fenced in, in spite of her years.
Something in her did not love a wall.

Her parting shot as I handed her over,
her poor bowels voided themselves
like the bad smell between us
which I took back with me without a word.

Sacred household

Breakfasting on this balcony in Crete,
biting into a sesame-seeded twist,
the taste of it takes me fifty years back

to my grandmother's tiptoe-high bed; wedged
between her pink viyella hip and my mother's bonier blue,
the warmth of their bodies, their talk lapping over my head.

The exact crumbling mouthful of the morning
penny biscuit and tea in bed,
of certainty amid doubt, luxury amid make-do.

Like a Minoan matriarch, bathed in attar of roses,
my grandmother's crepe soft skin, her amethysts
and rubies, riches and rituals, her steadfast régime.

Drawing us, willing or no, to daily prayer
to turn the Key to the Scriptures, follow the path
inscribed by her Mrs Eddy, to spiritual truth.

Still there in this mouthful: preparing the time-honoured way
for another sunrise; spreading the cloth;
laying the table the night before; setting the tray.

The smell of loose tea in silver-lined wooden boxes,
Indian and China mixed by my grandfather's hand,
victoria sponge and madeira mixed by hers.

The peas and runner beans he trained and we picked,
the roses he tended for her: Picadilly, Peace, Ma Perkins, Penelope…
My grandparents, body and soul in this bite, as I look out on the Libyan sea.

Grace

Gooseflesh in the shower
eyes closed it could be anywhere

except for the ring on my finger,
my hair, the fat on my hips,

except for the smell
of pure water, running seamless

telling me, woman
do not waste me, do not waste this well.

The Airing Cupboard

Secluded there, enveloped in the dark,
familiar sleeves brushing my face
and deeper in, the airy breath of sheets
waiting to be spread.
Worn shoes at my feet
and still the flow of my father's 78s reached in –
Some day I'm gonna write
The story of my life …
He never did.
Worked all hours to send us out
like boats down the Lough
into the world
out of that loamy dark.